When School Bells Call

∞ A True Story ∞

By Elva Hurst

WHEN SCHOOL BELLS CALL

Farm Life Series No. 2

ISBN 978-0-9815205-1-3

Printed in the USA
Manufactured by Thomson-Shore, Dexter, MI (USA);
RMA587AF722, January, 2013

First Printing, 2008

Publishing Services By:

Silver Line
PUBLISHING and BINDERY

510 Sleepy Hollow Road, Lititz, PA 17543 • (717) 627-3090

"Thanks," Josiah, for all the time you put into typing the manuscript. To my three other children — Bethany, Annie, and Jon — "thanks for drawing" the stories out of me. Your interest and ideas have inspired me to write. "God Bless" my husband, Ray for his kindness and patience when I should have been dusting furniture and sweeping floors instead of writing!

CONTENTS

SEPTEMBER IS HERE ...

"September is here, with its bright days of cheer, and we answer the school bells glad call," sang Mom as she braided my long light brown hair. It was indeed a bright and beautiful day, but cheer wasn't exactly what I felt. The feeling was a mixture of worry and dread. Mom called this recipe of emotions "anxiety." Worried questions swirled in my mind: *"What will school be like in the fifth grade?"* I had heard that fifth grade was much harder than fourth grade. *"Will our new teacher be nice? Will she give me the extra help I needed to learn?"*

Learning was difficult for me, and already I dreaded to see poor grades on my report card. "My stomach aches," I complained to Mom. She fixed me a cup of peppermint tea. *"That feels better already,"* I thought as I sipped on the hot liquid. Mom's caring gesture gave me courage to face a new grade in school.

We had a long walk to our one-room schoolhouse. I didn't have to walk alone. My sister, Eva Mae, who was two grades above me, walked with me. Together we stopped at the neighbor's lane, and met with Linda Reiff and her sisters.

Seeing Linda also helped to lift my spirits, and so did listening to the cheery songs of the birds and the rippling sound of the water as we crossed over the bridge at the creek near our house. Autumn was coming. There would be no more swimming in the creek or pony cart adventures. Linda and I laughed as we recalled our unforgettable pony cart ride to town and coming back in a thunder storm.

As we approached the school I could see classmates gathering from all directions. The Hoovers came from the west over the field behind the schoolhouse. From the north came our Amish neighbors, the Lapps. Just as we entered the school yard the big iron bell atop the schoolhouse roof rang out in three long, loud dongs. Its ringing did somewhat have a glad calling sound to it just as Mom's song described this morning. The anxious feelings gradually faded away.

Inside the schoolhouse, those familiar school smells greeted me. They were a combination of chalk, hardwood floor, and old wooden desks. "Good morning, Becky." I greeted another friend in the coatroom as I hung my sweater on the hook with my name. I set my lunchbox on a shelf in the back of the classroom and slid into a desk in the fourth row.

Our desks were old-fashioned wooden desks with a small hole, called an inkwell, in the upper right corner of the desktop. It held the ink bottle in the days long ago when schoolchildren did their schoolwork with quill and ink. The first row of desks had six small desks for the first graders. The desks in the other rows were bigger for the older children.

Other than sitting in a different row and having a new teacher, nothing had changed since last year. The vinyl window shades were pulled halfway down over the windows on either side of the classroom. I looked forward to eighth grade. Not only would that be my last year of school, but I would also get to sit at a desk by the window. The left back corner of the classroom had a shelf which held the water cooler. There we washed our hands before lunch since our school didn't have indoor plumbing. Our water came from a hand pump behind the schoolhouse. In the morning someone filled the large Thermos with water for the day.

In the back corner was our library—a large book case filled with rows of books. This was my favorite spot! *I hope the new teacher brought some new books, since I have read most every book in our small library more than once!* I thought. In the center front of the classroom sat the teachers' desk. On top of the teacher's desk, sat a small globe and a small bell with a neat row of books between. We didn't address our teacher by her name. We referred to her simply as "Teacher."

I glanced at the chalkboard behind her desk. **WELCOME BACK TO SCHOOL!** she had written in very neat and large lettering. Beneath that she wrote the assignments for the day and the classroom rules. I looked down at the pile of fifth-grade books on my desk. I saw a vocabulary book, spelling book, a black and white composition book for penmanship, geography, history, and arithmetic books.

I swallowed hard. The feeling of dread returned with more force than before at the sight of the arithmetic book. I disliked arithmetic very much! Children in public schools called it math. I wondered, *"Is theirs easier?"* Pushing aside the dread, I turned to see who sat behind me. *"Oh, dear,"* I thought, *"It is a boy!"*

I greeted a few more classmates, and we chatted until Teacher rang the small bell on her desk. We called this the second bell. We all quieted down quickly, eager to receive instructions for our new class. But first, we all rose, and stood by our desks, and prayed the Lord's Prayer. In fact, we did that every morning of each day of every school year.

"Our Father which art in heaven, hallowed be thy name. Thy kingdom come. Thy will be done in earth, as it is in heaven. Give us this day our daily bread. And forgive us our debts, as we forgive our debtors. And lead us not into temptation, but deliver us from evil. For thine is the kingdom, and the power, and the glory, for ever. Amen."

Teacher had a few words of welcome, and then she explained the rules and the consequences if we disobeyed them.

1. No running in the classroom
2. No chewing gum
3. No cheating
4. No whispering in class

She also encouraged us to talk only in English on the playground. We all spoke Pennsylvania Dutch at home. We needed to practice our English speaking skills. If we were caught talking in Dutch, our paper parrot on the wall would have one of his crackers taken away. If, at the end of the month, he still had all his crackers, Teacher would reward us with a prize!

The day went on rather slowly, I thought. To me the first day of school seemed longer than other days since we just had summer vacation and were not used to sitting for such a long time. About the third period I spied a note being passed around. It appeared to have started in the eighth-grade row. *"Uh-Oh! If Teacher sees, someone will be in trouble,"* I thought. The note was coming my way. *"What should I do? Should I take it?"* I wondered.

I watched as Mary Ella, who sat in front of me, read it, grinned, and then passed the note to me! Teacher was busy helping a first

grader. I opened it: "Meet in the buggy sheds after school" it read, "do not pass to lower graders."

"*The buggy sheds! Why?*" I wondered as I carefully passed it to Edwin Hoover who sat behind me. I watched as the note stopped at the end of the fifth-grade row. Teacher never saw it! I felt a little guilty, but mostly curious!

SH-H-H... IT'S A SURPRISE

Just as soon as Teacher dismissed my row, I grabbed my lunchbox from off the shelf and headed for the back door, forgetting my sweater. I went straight to the buggy shed. Across the road from our school was an Old Order Mennonite church. On the north and west side of the churchyard stood two long, open-sided buggy sheds. The horses with their buggies were tied here during church services. The sheds protected them from the weather and shaded from the hot sun.

By the time I arrived, most of the upper graders had already gathered. Rachel Oberholtzer, a tall, dark-haired eighth grader spoke up first. "Did anyone follow you here?"

she asked. We checked by peeking through the cracks in the wooden boards of the shed. The lower grades were still being dismissed.

"Hurry and gather together over here," she whispered. "We don't have much time! This coming Friday," she quickly announced, "everybody bring a wrapped package for a food roll at twelve o'clock sharp. Make the package big and hard to open. When I blow the whistle, everybody scream and shout just as loudly as you can! Until then, act normal so no one will get suspicious. And don't breathe a word to the lower graders because they'll snitch. Any questions?"

"How are we going to hide a big package

from Teacher?" asked James, another eighth grader.

"Well, don't make it so big that it can't fit in your desk," replied Rachel. "Now hurry, be sure to exit the shed in different directions so no one gets suspicious!"

Quickly and quietly we dispersed. I felt all tingly with excitement. I loved food rolls!

Linda's sisters asked, "What were you doing in the buggy shed?"

"Oh, just talking to our friends," Linda answered casually.

At the bend in the road we said good-bye to the Lapps, and continued down the hill and over the bridge toward home. All the way I planned what I was going to put in my package. I would assemble it tonight and then hide it under my bed. *"Shall I wrap potatoes or red beets?"* I wondered. *"Or maybe a can of baked beans. I'll see what Mom has in the cellar. I know, I'll take the label off the can and then it will really be a surprise package for Teacher,"* I schemed.

Food rolls were a tradition kept up in the private one-room schools. Teachers were usually young single girls who supported themselves. Often the schools were small, so the teachers didn't get a large salary. Food rolls helped to supply the teacher with food for the coming winter.

I could hardly wait for Friday to come. As

we approached the Reiff's lane, I reminded Linda not to share her secret and said good-bye.

At the house Mother asked, "How did the first day of school go?"

"Fine," I responded absent-mindedly. I grabbed my snack and hurried to change out of my school clothes. *"Let's see,"* I thought to myself, *"I need to help Mom with the supper and then help Dad milk the cows. Then I will be free to work on the package."*

During milking time I usually had plenty of time to think, so I tried to think of a clever way to package the food. When I caught sight of a bundle of baler string hanging by the barn wall, I thought, *"That's it! I'll layer my package with baler string between layers of brown paper and duct tape! That should help to consume time. Maybe Teacher will skip some classes if enough of us make unwrapping our packages difficult."* I mused and smiled smugly to myself.

It took me till bedtime to wrap a can of pineapples and a can of baked beans.

In the days that followed I concentrated on working hard in class and acting normal. Several times I caught myself just in time to keep from sharing our secret surprise.

Friday morning I pulled the package out from under my bed. "How am I going to get it to school without the younger ones noticing?" I asked. Eva Mae suggested a great idea. "Put it in the bottom of a book bag with books on top."

"That's a great idea!" I exclaimed.

In the coat-room at school, half a dozen normal-acting upper graders gathered, whispering in hushed voices. "How are we going to slip our packages into our desks without Teacher noticing?"

Mary Ella whispered loudly, "She's headed for the outhouse!" We walked normally to our desks, glad for the chance to put the packages in our desks unnoticed.

I shoved my package in the back corner of my desk, sat down, and waited for Teacher to return and ring the second bell. On the playground during first recess, we tried not to discuss our plan too much and arouse suspicion.

Rachel reminded us, "Now, remember, nobody do anything until I give the signal, and be ready."

Back in class I watched the clock. Eleven o'clock, eleven-thirty. Slower and slower it seemed to go as I waited impatiently for the big hand to reach twelve o'clock. I glanced around the room; everything seemed normal.

When Teacher walked toward her desk to put her books away and announce lunch, Rachel blew a sharp, long blast on her whistle.

We screamed at the top of our lungs, all the while rolling our packages down the aisle toward Teacher's desk.

Teacher turned pale and ran for the window, and throwing it open wide and hanging her head out gasping for air.

"Oh dear, she looks like she will faint." I thought to myself.

Before long she realized what was going on. We quieted down, and she sank into her chair and thanked us weakly.

Packages lay everywhere. The boys gathered them up and stacked them on Teacher's desk.

She told us to get our lunchboxes and eat while she unwrapped the packages. Our plan had been successful. Unwrapping the packages took her a long time! It took her the longest time to undo Jesse Martin's package. He had wrapped it with wire. Wire was a good choice because it protected the sweet potatoes inside.

Some one found a big box in the furnace room. Teacher filled it with cans of fruit and vegetables, cabbages, red beets, carrots, and much more. The lower grades had grown tired of watching and went outside to play. It took Teacher all the way to third recess to unwrap her gifts. We skipped that recess and had one more class. Then Teacher thanked us all again and dismissed us for the day.

All the way home we chatted about the fun and excitement of yet another successful food roll.

And So Goes Arithmetic!

My heart should have been glad, because we were right in the middle of my most favorite season of the year—autumn—and on the farm it was harvest time! The bright colors of autumn that usually cheered me were now overshadowed by those feelings of anxiety that followed me in my continued struggle with arithmetic!

Long division isn't hard to understand. Multiplying and dividing fractions isn't too bad either. But what I do despise the most is reading problems! I just can't comprehend what they are trying to teach me. Maybe the writers of these problems are only trying to trick me. I'll ask Mom to help me," I decided.

Mom tried to help me but couldn't seem to understand them either. It seemed that I had lost her somewhere back in fourth grade arithmetic! Last year I had tried throwing my arithmetic paper with poor grades on them into the creek that ran under the bridge near our house, but that didn't work. Poor grades just showed up again later in my report card.

When I asked other members of my family to help me, they just called me a dummy. That hurt me deeply. For years to come, those words haunted me whenever I was faced with something new and difficult. I'd hear the words in my head, *"You can't do it because you're a dummy."* Unfortunately, I too often believed them. It wasn't until later in life that I discovered what God said about me. When I believed God's Word rather than thinking I was a dummy, I received freedom; and I was no longer controlled by those negative thoughts.

After school my brother Marvin asked, "Would you like to go squirrel hunting with me?"

"I suppose that would help get my mind off arithmetic," I figured. I followed him through the drying meadow grass. He carried the .22 rifle over his shoulder as he headed for the woods by the creek that ran through our property.

The day was summerlike. *Indian summer*, Dad called it. A warm spell in the middle of cooler autumn days. Colors of autumn were everywhere. Leaves, the yellow of squash and the orange of pumpkins, set against the blue of the sky warmed my heart indeed.

Just then we heard a rustle in the leaves. We stopped in our tracks and stood still. Sure enough, a squirrel scampered up a nearby sycamore tree. Marvin raised the gun, took aim, and *CRACK!* He got the squirrel with a single shot.

"Your turn," he grinned.

He loaded the gun, handed it to me, and gave me a quick lesson about aimin' and pullin' triggers. We walked on as quietly as we could in the dry, fallen leaves and the underbrush of the woods.

"There," he whispered, pointing to a maple tree by the line fence.

Raising the gun up to my shoulder, I aimed just as he had instructed me. There, through the scope of the gun, I saw a handsome squirrel. He was sitting on the branch with his tail twitching and head turning from side to side.

"He senses danger," I thought. All around him were golden yellow leaves, patches of blue sky, and the warm sunlight streaming through the opening in the brush of the maple tree. All

was quiet and still. Not even a breath of wind stirred the leaves.

"Thump, thump, thump," went my heart. *"Be still and pull the trigger,"* I told myself, but my fingers refused to move!

"I just can't do it," I confessed to my brother, and I put the gun down.

"What's the matter with you?" he sputtered. "Give me that gun!" he demanded angrily as he grabbed the gun and took aim. But the squirrel had already run away.

I felt good and bad at the same time. Good for letting the squirrel escape and bad for disappointing my brother. On and on he scolded me for letting it get away. However, before long he spied another squirrel. *CRACK!* the squirrel dropped dead.

Satisfied with his hunt he turned back to the farm. Squirrel meat is delicious, but I don't like skinning them. Somehow, Marvin talked me into helping him again, muttering something about Mom needing meat for supper, and, if I didn't work, I shouldn't eat!

Meanwhile, Mom heated lard in a large cast-iron skillet and fried the two squirrels. The aroma of the frying meat mixed with the smell of tomato juice made my mouth water.

Mom had been canning tomato juice. Whenever Mom canned tomato juice we always had tomato soup for supper that night. Tomato soup was my favorite soup. I especially liked it when she drizzled homemade browned butter on top. *Mmmm.*

Coming home from a hunt in the woods on a beautiful autumn day to tomato soup with browned butter for supper was enough to help anyone forget arithmetic! Well . . . almost.

4

PLAYING HOOKY

"Today we're going to start picking corn," Dad announced to my brother at breakfast. I liked helping with the harvest but today was a school day and of course I would have to go to school. The morning was bright and cheery.

The sunrise promised another lovely autumn day, just right for a harvest-time walk through the fields. *"Perhaps I could tell Mom I'm not feeling well this morning,"* I thought to myself. *"Besides, there is going to be an arithmetic test at school today. Yes, that's what I'll do."* I decided.

It worked! "Perhaps you should stay home from school today," Mom said. I laid around the house until the breakfast dishes were washed

and then grabbed my sweater and slipped out the back door. *I'll walk through the corn rows that have already been harvested and enjoy all the sights and sounds of harvest time.* I liked hearing the cawing of the crows and honking of the

geese as they flew south over our fields to a nearby lake.

But my walk didn't go quite as I had planned. By the time I got outside, the sun had slipped behind the gathering clouds, and the light breeze was turning chilly. I shivered and buttoned up my sweater. A familiar feeling appeared from deep inside of me, a feeling that always showed up whenever I did something wrong—guilt. I had lied to Mom, and now my conscience troubled me.

No longer was I enjoying my harvest-time walk. I made my way across the field anyway, looking for corncobs the picker had missed. About halfway through my walk, I decided to turn around and go back to the farmhouse. *"Sin spoils the fun,"* I realized. *"I won't do this again! Tomorrow I must go back to school."*

After the evening milking, I helped Dad unload ear corn by climbing into the bin wagon and pushing the ears with my feet toward the small opening at the bottom of the wagon. Outside the opening, Dad guided the ears into a blower grinder that chopped the corn, cob and all into tiny bits and pieces and blew it up into the silo. There it was stored during the wintertime. We fed it to the cows each day.

The cornstalks, now dead and dry, lay flat in the field. Later Dad would chop, rake and bale the stalks. These bales we called corn fodder, which made good bedding for the cows on the cold winter days. For now we would stack them in the haymow along with the hay we had already baled during the summer. Sometimes on rainy days, we would go into the haymow and build tunnels and huts with the bales.

Before returning to the house, Dad reminded me to pen up the turkeys. "Turkeys can't see well in the dark, so it is best to do it while there is still daylight." During the day, the turkeys were allowed to be out in the meadow. There they would feed on bugs and grass. Then in the evening it was my job to chase them back into the pen. I also made sure they had plenty of water. But, one can't chase turkeys very well. Whenever I tried, they would only turn aside, stand there and look at me with their beady eyes and make annoying turkey sounds! I soon figured out that they would follow me or another turkey. So I would get their attention and walk towards the pen, gobbling like a turkey!

The pen had a small doghouse-like opening, I taught them how to get through it by crawling through the small opening myself! It was a tight squeeze, but it worked! "Gobble, Gobble!" I squawked as they followed me into the pen. But turkeys are not very smart; I had to teach them this lesson over and over again.

Sometimes my brothers and sisters called each other a dumb turkey. Now I knew why. *"Turkeys really are dumb!" I thought. It seems as though they refuse to learn.* "Well," I thought, *"I'm not going to be a dumb turkey. I learned my lesson today, and I will not forget it. Lying is not smart!"*

Thanksgiving wasn't very far away, and the turkeys were getting bigger by the day. We would soon sell most of them, but some we would butcher for the freezer. The nice plump one would be kept for our Thanksgiving dinner!

I wished, however, it was our nasty "little" red rooster going to the chopping block instead of the big turkey. The rooster had floddered me one too many times, and I had it in for him!

5

HARVEST MOON

It was Friday and I was glad for a new day. While walking to school I prayed a prayer I had found from a card and memorized the evening before. It helped me to express what I was feeling: "God, You've ushered in another day untouched and fresh and new, so here I am to ask you God if You'll renew me too. Forgive the many errors that I made yesterday, and put it in my heart to walk closer in Your way."

It felt good to my heart to pray those words. I was also glad it was Friday. "Today is the day Teacher asked the upper grade girls to stay after school to help with the fall school cleaning." I remembered excitedly. "At last I am old enough to help."

After the younger students were dismissed, the upper grade girls gathered around Teacher's desk while she assigned us jobs two by two. To some she gave the task of wiping desks, to others washing windows. Armed with buckets and brooms, Mary Ella and I marched to our assignment: the outhouse! When we lifted the latch, the creaky door slowly swung open. We stood in the doorway and surveyed the job. I stopped and stared at the bees' nest in the rafters.

First we took our brooms and knocked the bees' nest down, crashed spider webs and swept out dry leaves and dirt. "It hardly seems like work at all," I told Mary Ella. We were having fun. As we worked we talked and laughed and shared secrets. "Mary Ella, I'm going to tell you a secret, but you must promise not to tell anyone," I warned.

"Okay, I won't tell," she promised.

"I am going to be an aunt," I told her. "My oldest sister Vera is going to have a baby!"

"Wow!" she exclaimed, "That's exciting!"

Together we scrubbed down the seats and floor. Last of all, we replaced the old rolls of toilet paper. While doing so, I remembered Mom once told me that when she was a girl, there was no such thing as soft toilet paper in the outhouses. Instead, people used crumpled-up newspaper or pages from old catalogs or magazines. I couldn't help but wonder how that worked.

Soon we joined the other teams inside the schoolhouse. Together, we shared the biggest job of all: sweeping and washing down the hardwood floor of the classroom. The schoolhouse smelled fresh and clean, now we were ready for a new season.

Teacher thanked us all by treating us with yummy homemade cream-filled chocolate cupcakes and red punch. To have finished such a large task gave us a good feeling inside. It took us only a little over an hour to accomplish the cleaning. The walk home was refreshing. Autumn was coming to a close. The fields were now bare and the days were getting shorter and cooler.

We took a few minutes to stop by the neighbor's pasture and say hi to Tony, the pony. Every afternoon he waited for us by the fence and whinnied, hoping for a treat from our lunchboxes. We saved our bread crusts and apple cores for him. We watched him eat it, stroked his forehead, and then continued down the hill toward home.

Later that evening, my family worked together to gather the last of the garden vegetables. Busily, I pulled the remaining beets from the damp soil. The evening was still, clear, and chilly. The birds quieted down their singing. There remained only the sound of a few crickets and the occasional croak of a bullfrog from down by the creek bank.

But then I heard it—the best harvest-time sound of all, a sound I shall never forget. Way faroff in the distance, an old steam engine blew its whistle: *Whooo-a-whooooo*. I stopped pulling beets and stood quietly, straining to hear it again. I loved that sound, and it was coming closer and closer.

Soon I could see it from our garden all the way across our meadow, to the road beyond the creek. The old steam engine was slowly making its way up the hill, traveling from one Amish farm to another. I could barely see it in the fading light of the evening. Black smoke rose from the smokestack every time the whistle blew.

Dad had told me once that when he was nine years old, the steam engine was at his family's farm to steam tobacco beds. Grandpa said, "Do not pull the whistle because it will scare the chickens." Later that night, Dad pulled

the whistle, but it got stuck and wouldn't stop blowing. For nearly an hour the whistle blew! Grandpa and the other men put cotton in their ears and tied a feed sack around the whistle to muffle the sound. They tried everything to make it stop blowing. Finally, as a last resort, one of the men whacked it good with a hammer. It worked! The whistle stopped blowing.

In the garden, the sounds of the whistle had faded again as the steam engine continued down the road. When I turned back to pull more beets, what I saw next I will never forget either. Away in the east, across the open fields, rose the biggest, brightest, roundest harvest moon I had ever seen.

The others had gone to the house with a load of potatoes for the cellar. The remaining light of sunset was fading in the west, and the sounds of the whistle still lingered in my ears. I was left alone—alone, with the moon, the stars, and the music of a late autumn evening—alone with God. The night was cool, but the earth felt warm to my bare feet, and my heart was warmed by all the beauty of God's creation.

My soul was beginning to realize the goodness of God's loving care for me. Teacher had noticed I liked to draw, and she encouraged me to paint. *"Maybe someday I'll be an artist, and paint all the beautiful things God created for us to enjoy."* I thought to myself.

As for arithmetic . . . Mom had said, "Just do your best and leave the rest." I decided that night, I would pray and trust God with my problems. Mom had also said, "Who trusts does not worry; who worries, does not trust." I chose to trust God instead of worrying, and that's how Mom helped me with arithmetic!

GLOSSARY

Amish

A seventeenth century group of Swiss Mennonites, led by Jacob Amman, who broke away from the Mennonites and formed the Old Order Amish Church. They use horses for farming and transportation. They dress in a simple manner and forbid electricity and telephones.

Arithmetic

Whole numbers used to add and subtract, multiply and divide. Otherwise known as *math* (short for arithmetic)

Haymow

An area in the upper level of the barn where bales are stacked and stored for the winter

Lard

Fat from pigs that is melted down and used in cooking

Line fence

A fence that marks the boundary line between one farm and another

Old Order Mennonites

A branch of the Mennonite Church whose lifestyle is similar to the Amish in tradition and transportation. They also use a horse and buggy for travel.

One-room school

A school building that has only one classroom, where all eight grades are educated

Outhouse

A small shed outback used as an outdoor toilet

Playing hooky

To stay away from school without honest permission

Tradition

The practice of beliefs and customs handed down for generations over many years

Steam engine

An engine that uses steam to run its mechanical parts

Supper

What county folks call the evening meal

ECIPES

Tomato Soup

1 quart tomato juice (home canned tastes better)
2 quarts milk (raw milk is best)
1 teaspoon of salt
A little pepper

Pour tomato juice in kettle. Add milk, salt, and
pepper. Turn stove on and heat but do not boil.
Pour browned butter on top and serve.

Note: some add other spices such as onion and
garlic powder and maybe a little basil, but we just
season ours with salt and pepper. Sometimes we
dice hard-boiled eggs and add that to the soup in
our bowl along with a few crackers. Yum!

Browned Butter

Melt 2 tablespoons butter in a small frying pan
(Do not use margarine).
Fry until butter turns a little brown—watch carefully; it can burn quickly. Drizzle on the soup in the kettle. Enjoy!

Also Written and Illustrated
by Elva Hurst

The Story of Woolly My Pet Lamb

To order books and visit
Elva's Barnyard Art
Gallery online, go to
www.elvaschalkart.com

You can also write to:

Barnyard Art
1519 Brunnerville Rd.
Lititz, Pa 17543

Middle Creek School

Elva in the 8th grade.

Millway Mennonite
Church and buggy shed.

Middle Creek School
students, 1982.